LIVEWIRE
REAL LIVES

Britney Spears

Mike Wilson

Published in association with The Basic Skills Agency

Hodder & Stoughton

A MEMBER OF THE HODDER HEADLINE GROUP

Acknowledgements
Cover: Mitchell Gerber/Corbis

*Photos: pp iv, 19 © Alpha; pp 4, 8, 14 © Reuters NewMedia Inc./Corbis; p 11 ©
'PA'News; p 24 © Retna; p 26 © Redferns*

Every effort has been made to trace copyright holders of material reproduced in this book.
Any rights not acknowledged will be acknowledged in subsequent printings if notice is
given to the publisher.

Orders: please contact Bookpoint Ltd, 78 Milton Park, Abingdon, Oxon OX14 4TD.
Telephone (44) 01235 827720, Fax: (44) 01235 400454. Lines are open from 9.00–6.00,
Monday to Saturday, with a 24 hour message answering service.
Email address: orders@bookpoint.co.uk

British Library Cataloguing in Publication Data
A catalogue record for this title is available from The British Library

ISBN 0 340 80084 4

First published 2001
Impression number   10 9 8 7 6 5 4 3 2 1
Year   2007 2006 2005 2004 2003 2002 2001

Typeset by SX Composing DTP, Rayleigh, Essex
Printed in Great Britain for Hodder & Stoughton Educational, a division of Hodder Headline
Plc, 338 Euston Road, London NW1 3BH by Redwood Books, Trowbridge, Wilts.

Contents

Britney Spears made $15 million dollars by the time she was 18!

This is the story
of a young girl
from Louisiana, USA.

How she grew up.
How she became a young woman.
How she tried
to make sense of the world.

Just like all the other girls.

Except she wasn't like all the other girls.
She had been a TV star
from the age of 11.
By the time she was 18,
she'd made 15 million dollars.

This is the story
of Britney Spears.

1 Home

Britney's home
is Kentwood, Louisiana.

Kentwood is a small town.
Only 1,200 people live there.

Britney was born there
on 2 December 1981.

Her dad, Jamie,
and her mum, Lynne,
are Baptists.

'God has a plan for all of us,'
Britney says.
'Mine is to be a singer.'

2 The Mickey Mouse Years

Britney began to dance
as soon as she could stand up.
She has been singing
since she was five years old.
She won her first talent contest
when she was six.

When she was eight,
she went to a dance school
in New York.
She was given parts in plays
and in TV ads.

Then she got a place
on Disney's TV show,
The Mickey Mouse Club.

She was 11 years old.

Britney and Christina now have to compete with each other
for chart success.

Britney had a friend
on the show.
Her name was Christina Aguilera.

Christina was a year older
than Britney – she was 12.
Britney and Christina
were the two babies on the show.

Now they are both world-famous
they don't stay in touch.
They only meet at awards
and photo shoots.

'It was so good to see her,'
says Britney.
'We chatted
and had a laugh
about the press we were getting.'

So it seems the stories
that Britney and Christina fell out
were just stories.

Britney spent two years
in *The Mickey Mouse Club*.

After that,
she went back home
to Kentwood.
She went to high school.
She tried to settle down.

She couldn't do it.
'I need to sing,' said Britney,
'and I love to travel.'

So she went back to New York.
She was hoping
to make it big in pop.

Sometimes, life was hard.
Sometimes the family was poor.
They could not always afford
to pay the bills.

Then, in 1998,
Britney's dream came true.

'Baby One More Time'
was written for the pop band TLC.
They didn't want it.
So Britney got to record the song instead.
She was 17.

In the video,
Britney danced around high school
in a sexy school uniform.
She wore a short skirt,
and a tight white shirt,
singing 'Hit me baby,
one more time!'

She looked young and innocent,
– but sexy and not so innocent –
all at the same time!

Britney's first song 'Baby One More Time', was a huge hit.

The song was pure 'adult teen' pop.
It was a huge hit.

In the UK,
it sold half a million copies
in the first week.

Britney was the youngest star ever
to be at Number 1
in America and Britain
at the same time.

3 The Big Time

Suddenly,
Britney was world famous.

Baby One More Time
got to Number 1
in the UK album charts.
It sold over seven million copies
all over the world.

Britney's second album
Oops! . . . I Did It Again
sold 1.3 million copies
in the first week.

Britney won four awards at the 1999 MTV Europe
Music Awards.

In 1999
she won four US Billboard Awards,
and four MTV Awards:

– best pop act
– best female performer
– best new act
– best song.

Britney was in the Top Ten websites
looked up on the World Wide Web.

4   Sex and Religion

In the video for 'Oops!'
Britney wore a tight red cat suit.
She sang, 'I'm not that innocent . . .'
Later she was on the cover
of *Rolling Stone* magazine.
She was lying in bed,
holding a Tellytubby,
dressed only in bra and pants.

That month,
Rolling Stone magazine
had record sales . . .

Was Britney using sex
to sell more records
and more magazines?

Britney likes to wear sexy outfits.

She was still only a teenager.
It was like she was a young girl
and a sexy young woman
all at the same time.

Was it right
for Britney (aged 17)
to be so child-like
and so sexy?

Britney just blushes
and says:
'It's not me!
It's just a part I play
for the camera.

'Just because I look sexy
for *Rolling Stone*,
it doesn't mean I'm a bad girl.

'I come from the south,'
she explains.
'It's real hot down there.
We wear less clothes
and think nothing of it.'

In real life,
Britney is quiet and shy.

She blushes and giggles
when she talks about Justin
from N' Sync.

'He's the cutest thing in the world,'
she says.
'We talk all the time,
but we're not dating.
We just hang out.'

Britney believes in God.
She believes it's wrong
to have sex before you get married.

She says:
'If I did anything else,
it would be a mistake.'

In June 2000,
a man offered £7.5 million
to sleep with Britney.

Britney said:
'That's disgusting!
He should go and have a cold shower
and leave me alone!'

But then Britney says:
'Sometimes I want to show off more of my body,
but the record company doesn't like me to,
because of what people say.
That's bad.
I should be able to show off my feminine side.'

Normal, shy little girl next door?
Saving herself for the right man?
Or sexy young woman,
who likes to show off her body?

Sometimes
it seems hard to tell
which is the real Britney Spears.

5   The Real Britney Spears

It's true that Britney can be
just like any other teenager.

She likes clothes and shopping.
She likes romantic movies.
She likes Madonna,
and Mariah Carey.
She likes pizza and pasta,
and ice-cream.

She likes hanging out with friends.
She likes to lay out
on a beach somewhere,
getting a tan.
She still feels awkward
when she meets somebody famous
or somebody good looking.

Britney still likes to hang out with her friends.

Britney had her belly button pierced,
and she'd really like a tattoo.
But she knows that her mother
(and the record company)
would probably go mad!

Because of her work
and her lifestyle
Britney feels older than 18.
But she says
she still acts like an idiot sometimes!

6 Queen Britney?

Prince William is a big fan.
He is the same age as Britney.

He wants to meet her
when she comes to the UK.

The Prince has written to her
and Britney wrote back.
She sent him her CD
and some of her photos.

'He's very cute,'
Britney told one magazine,
'and he's very, very sweet.
I'd love to meet him.'

'I'd like to buy a house in London,'
she went on,
'but I'm not planning
to live next door to Prince William!'

That's good news
for William's father, Prince Charles.
He says he doesn't want
to be a grandfather just yet!

7   Heart to Heart

After non-stop touring,
Britney found time to write a book.

She put it together
with her mum, Lynne.

It's the story
of Britney's rise to fame.
It's also the story
of Britney and her mum.

Did her mother push Britney too hard
when she was little?

'No,' says Britney.
'I've seen stage mums,
and my mum is nothing like that.
It's always been about
what I wanted to do.'

Lynne is Britney's mum.
She is also her best friend.

Their book is called *Heart to Heart*.

Britney's mum is also her best friend.

A man from the record company
sums up Britney Spears:
'She is the girl next door,'
he says.

'Every girl wants to be like her.
Every guy wants to be with her
and get to know her.
Britney has kid appeal.'

In May 2000,
Britney was voted
'Best Person To Go On Holiday With'
by the kids who watch the Disney Channel.

So Britney still has kid appeal,
but she has sex appeal as well.

Britney's music appeals to everyone.

In 1999,
she was voted
Sexiest Woman of the Year
by one magazine.

'I want to be a legend,' Britney says,
'like Madonna.
This is what I pray for every day.

'God has led me everywhere,' she says.
'I thank him for it.'